ODOUR OF CHRYSANTHEMUMS

D H LAWRENCE:

TEXT AND ANALYSIS

Dog's Tail Books

ISBN: 978-1517426507

www.dogstailbooks.co.uk

Odour of Chrysanthemums

I

The small locomotive engine, Number 4, came clanking, stumbling down from Selston--with seven full waggons. It appeared round the corner with loud threats of speed, but the colt that it startled from among the gorse, which still flickered indistinctly in the raw afternoon, outdistanced it at a canter. A woman, walking up the railway line to Underwood, drew back into the hedge, held her basket aside, and watched the footplate of the engine advancing. The trucks thumped heavily past, one by one, with slow inevitable movement, as she stood insignificantly trapped between the jolting black waggons and the hedge; then they curved away towards the coppice where the withered oak leaves dropped noiselessly, while the birds, pulling at the scarlet hips beside the track, made off into the dusk that had already crept into the spinney. In the open, the smoke from the engine sank and cleaved to the rough grass. The fields were dreary and forsaken, and in the marshy strip that led to the whimsey, a reedy pit-pond, the fowls had already abandoned their run among the alders, to roost in the tarred fowl-house. The pit-bank loomed up beyond the pond, flames like red sores licking its ashy sides, in the afternoon's stagnant light. Just beyond rose the tapering chimneys and the clumsy black head-stocks of Brinsley Colliery. The two wheels were spinning fast up against the sky, and the winding-engine rapped out its little spasms. The miners were being turned up.

The engine whistled as it came into the wide bay of railway lines beside the colliery, where rows of trucks stood in harbour.

Miners, single, trailing and in groups, passed like shadows diverging home. At the edge of the ribbed level of sidings squat a low cottage, three steps down from the cinder track. A large bony vine clutched at the house, as if to claw down the tiled roof. Round the bricked yard grew a few wintry primroses. Beyond, the long garden sloped down to a bush-covered brook course. There were some twiggy apple trees, winter-crack trees, and ragged cabbages. Beside the path hung dishevelled pink chrysanthemums, like pink cloths hung on bushes. A woman came stooping out of the felt-covered fowl-house, half-way down the garden. She closed and padlocked the door, then drew herself erect, having brushed some bits from her white apron.

She was a tall woman of imperious mien, handsome, with definite black eyebrows. Her smooth black hair was parted exactly. For a few moments she stood steadily watching the miners as they passed along the railway: then she turned towards the brook course. Her face was calm and set, her mouth was closed with disillusionment. After a moment she called:

"John!" There was no answer. She waited, and then said distinctly:

"Where are you?"

"Here!" replied a child's sulky voice from among the bushes. The woman looked piercingly through the dusk.

"Are you at that brook?" she asked sternly.

For answer the child showed himself before the raspberry-canes that rose like whips. He was a small, sturdy boy of five. He stood quite still, defiantly.

"Oh!" said the mother, conciliated. "I thought you were down at that wet brook--and you remember what I told you--"

The boy did not move or answer.

"Come, come on in," she said more gently, "it's getting dark. There's your grandfather's engine coming down the line!"

The lad advanced slowly, with resentful, taciturn movement. He was dressed in trousers and waistcoat of cloth that was too thick and hard for the size of the garments. They were evidently cut down from a man's clothes.

As they went slowly towards the house he tore at the ragged wisps of chrysanthemums and dropped the petals in handfuls along the path.

"Don't do that--it does look nasty," said his mother. He refrained, and she, suddenly pitiful, broke off a twig with three or four wan flowers and held them against her face. When mother and son reached the yard her hand hesitated, and instead of laying the flower aside, she pushed it in her apron-band. The mother and son stood at the foot of the three steps looking across the bay of lines at the passing home of the miners. The trundle of the small train was imminent. Suddenly the engine loomed past the house and came to a stop opposite the gate.

The engine-driver, a short man with round grey beard, leaned out of the cab high above the woman.

"Have you got a cup of tea?" he said in a cheery, hearty fashion.

It was her father. She went in, saying she would mash. Directly, she returned.

"I didn't come to see you on Sunday," began the little grey-bearded man.

"I didn't expect you," said his daughter.

The engine-driver winced; then, reassuming his cheery, airy manner, he said:

"Oh, have you heard then? Well, and what do you think--?"

"I think it is soon enough," she replied.

At her brief censure the little man made an impatient gesture, and said coaxingly, yet with dangerous coldness:

"Well, what's a man to do? It's no sort of life for a man of my years, to sit at my own hearth like a stranger. And if I'm going to marry again it may as well be soon as late--what does it matter to anybody?"

The woman did not reply, but turned and went into the house. The man in the engine-cab stood assertive, till she returned with a cup of tea and a piece of bread and butter on a plate. She went up the steps and stood near the footplate of the hissing engine.

"You needn't 'a' brought me bread an' butter," said her father. "But a cup of tea"--he sipped appreciatively--"it's very nice." He sipped for a moment or two, then: "I hear as Walter's got another bout on," he said.

"When hasn't he?" said the woman bitterly.

"I heered tell of him in the 'Lord Nelson' braggin' as he was going to spend that b---- afore he went: half a sovereign that was."

"When?" asked the woman.

"A' Sat'day night--I know that's true."

"Very likely," she laughed bitterly. "He gives me twenty-three shillings."

"Aye, it's a nice thing, when a man can do nothing with his money but make a beast of himself!" said the grey-whiskered man. The woman turned her head away. Her father swallowed the last of his tea and handed her the cup.

"Aye," he sighed, wiping his mouth. "It's a settler, it is--"

He put his hand on the lever. The little engine strained and groaned, and the train rumbled towards the crossing. The woman again looked across the metals. Darkness was settling over the spaces of the railway and trucks: the miners, in grey sombre groups, were still passing home. The winding-engine pulsed hurriedly, with brief pauses. Elizabeth Bates looked at the dreary flow of men, then she went indoors. Her husband did not come.

The kitchen was small and full of firelight; red coals piled glowing up the chimney mouth. All the life of the room seemed in the white, warm hearth and the steel fender reflecting the red fire. The cloth was laid for tea; cups glinted in the shadows. At the back, where the lowest stairs protruded into the room, the boy sat struggling with a knife and a piece of whitewood. He was almost hidden in the shadow. It was half-past four. They had but to await the father's coming to begin tea. As the mother watched her son's sullen little struggle with the wood, she saw herself in his silence and pertinacity; she saw the father in her child's indifference to all but himself. She seemed to be occupied by her husband. He had probably gone past his home, slunk past his own door, to drink before he came in, while his dinner spoiled and wasted in waiting. She glanced at the clock, then took the potatoes to strain them in the yard. The garden and fields beyond the brook were closed in uncertain darkness. When she rose with the saucepan, leaving the drain steaming into the night behind her, she saw the yellow lamps were lit along the high road that went up the hill away beyond the space of the railway lines and the field.

Then again she watched the men trooping home, fewer now and fewer.

Indoors the fire was sinking and the room was dark red. The woman put her saucepan on the hob, and set a batter pudding near the mouth of the oven. Then she stood unmoving. Directly, gratefully, came quick young steps to the door. Someone hung on the latch a moment, then a little girl entered and began pulling off her outdoor things, dragging a mass of curls, just ripening from gold to brown, over her eyes with her hat.

Her mother chid her for coming late from school, and said she would have to keep her at home the dark winter days.

"Why, mother, it's hardly a bit dark yet. The lamp's not lighted, and my father's not home."

"No, he isn't. But it's a quarter to five! Did you see anything of him?"

The child became serious. She looked at her mother with large, wistful blue eyes.

"No, mother, I've never seen him. Why? Has he come up an' gone past, to Old Brinsley? He hasn't, mother, 'cos I never saw him."

"He'd watch that," said the mother bitterly, "he'd take care as you didn't see him. But you may depend upon it, he's seated in the 'Prince o' Wales'. He wouldn't be this late."

The girl looked at her mother piteously.

"Let's have our teas, mother, should we?" said she.

The mother called John to table. She opened the door once more and looked out across the darkness of the lines. All was deserted: she could not hear the winding-engines.

"Perhaps," she said to herself, "he's stopped to get some ripping done."

They sat down to tea. John, at the end of the table near the door, was almost lost in the darkness. Their faces were hidden from each other. The girl crouched against the fender slowly moving a thick piece of bread before the fire. The lad, his face a dusky mark on the shadow, sat watching her who was transfigured in the red glow.

"I do think it's beautiful to look in the fire," said the child.

"Do you?" said her mother. "Why?"

"It's so red, and full of little caves--and it feels so nice, and you can fair smell it."

"It'll want mending directly," replied her mother, "and then if your father comes he'll carry on and say there never is a fire when a man comes home sweating from the pit.--A public-house is always warm enough."

There was silence till the boy said complainingly: "Make haste, our Annie."

"Well, I am doing! I can't make the fire do it no faster, can I?"

"She keeps wafflin' it about so's to make 'er slow," grumbled the boy.

"Don't have such an evil imagination, child," replied the mother.

Soon the room was busy in the darkness with the crisp sound of crunching. The mother ate very little. She drank her tea determinedly, and sat thinking. When she rose her anger was evident in the stern unbending of her head. She looked at the pudding in the fender, and broke out:

"It is a scandalous thing as a man can't even come home to his dinner! If it's crozzled up to a cinder I don't see why I should care. Past his very door he goes to get to a public-house, and here I sit with his dinner waiting for him--"

She went out. As she dropped piece after piece of coal on the red fire, the shadows fell on the walls, till the room was almost in total darkness.

"I canna see," grumbled the invisible John. In spite of herself, the mother laughed.

"You know the way to your mouth," she said. She set the dustpan outside the door. When she came again like a shadow on the hearth, the lad repeated, complaining sulkily:

"I canna see."

"Good gracious!" cried the mother irritably, "you're as bad as your father if it's a bit dusk!"

Nevertheless she took a paper spill from a sheaf on the mantelpiece and proceeded to light the lamp that hung from the ceiling in the middle of the room. As she reached up, her figure displayed itself just rounding with maternity.

"Oh, mother--!" exclaimed the girl.

"What?" said the woman, suspended in the act of putting the lamp glass over the flame. The copper reflector shone handsomely on her, as she stood with uplifted arm, turning to face her daughter.

"You've got a flower in your apron!" said the child, in a little rapture at this unusual event.

"Goodness me!" exclaimed the woman, relieved. "One would think the house was afire." She replaced the glass and waited a moment before turning up the wick. A pale shadow was seen floating vaguely on the floor.

"Let me smell!" said the child, still rapturously, coming forward and putting her face to her mother's waist.

"Go along, silly!" said the mother, turning up the lamp. The light revealed their suspense so that the woman felt it almost unbearable. Annie was still bending at her waist. Irritably, the mother took the flowers out from her apron-band.

"Oh, mother--don't take them out!" Annie cried, catching her hand and trying to replace the sprig.

"Such nonsense!" said the mother, turning away. The child put the pale chrysanthemums to her lips, murmuring:

"Don't they smell beautiful!"

Her mother gave a short laugh.

"No," she said, "not to me. It was chrysanthemums when I married him, and chrysanthemums when you were born, and the first time they ever brought him home drunk, he'd got brown chrysanthemums in his button-hole."

She looked at the children. Their eyes and their parted lips were wondering. The mother sat rocking in silence for some time. Then she looked at the clock.

"Twenty minutes to six!" In a tone of fine bitter carelessness she continued: "Eh, he'll not come now till they bring him. There he'll stick! But he needn't come rolling in here in his pit-dirt, for I won't wash him. He can lie on the floor--Eh, what a fool I've been, what a fool! And this is what I came here for, to this dirty hole, rats and all, for him to slink past his very door. Twice last week--he's begun now-"

She silenced herself, and rose to clear the table.

While for an hour or more the children played, subduedly intent, fertile of imagination, united in fear of the mother's wrath, and in dread of their father's home-coming, Mrs Bates sat in her rocking-chair making a 'singlet' of thick cream-coloured flannel, which gave a dull wounded sound as she tore off the grey edge. She worked at her sewing with energy, listening to the children, and her anger wearied itself, lay down to rest, opening its eyes from time to time and steadily watching, its ears raised to listen. Sometimes even her anger quailed and shrank, and the mother suspended her sewing, tracing the footsteps that thudded along the sleepers outside; she would lift her head sharply to bid the children 'hush', but she recovered herself in time, and the footsteps went past the gate, and the children were not flung out of their playing world.

But at last Annie sighed, and gave in. She glanced at her waggon of slippers, and loathed the game. She turned plaintively to her mother.

"Mother!"--but she was inarticulate.

John crept out like a frog from under the sofa. His mother glanced up.

"Yes," she said, "just look at those shirt-sleeves!"

The boy held them out to survey them, saying nothing. Then somebody called in a hoarse voice away down the line, and suspense bristled in the room, till two people had gone by outside, talking.

"It is time for bed," said the mother.

"My father hasn't come," wailed Annie plaintively. But her mother was primed with courage.

"Never mind. They'll bring him when he does come--like a log." She meant there would be no scene. "And he may sleep on the floor till he wakes himself. I know he'll not go to work tomorrow after this!"

The children had their hands and faces wiped with a flannel. They were very quiet. When they had put on their nightdresses, they said their prayers, the boy mumbling. The mother looked down at them, at the brown silken bush of intertwining curls in the nape of the girl's neck, at the little black head of the lad, and her heart burst with anger at their father who caused all three such distress. The children hid their faces in her skirts for comfort.

When Mrs Bates came down, the room was strangely empty, with a tension of expectancy. She took up her sewing and stitched for some time without raising her head. Meantime her anger was tinged with fear.

II

The clock struck eight and she rose suddenly, dropping her sewing on her chair. She went to the stairfoot door, opened it, listening. Then she went out, locking the door behind her.

Something scuffled in the yard, and she started, though she knew it was only the rats with which the place was overrun. The night was very dark. In the great bay of railway lines, bulked with trucks, there was no trace of light, only away back she could see a few yellow lamps at the pit-top, and the red smear of the burning pit-bank on the night. She hurried along the edge of the track, then, crossing the converging lines, came to the stile by the white gates, whence she emerged on the road. Then the fear which had led her shrank. People were walking up to New Brinsley; she saw the lights in the houses; twenty yards further on were the broad windows of the 'Prince of Wales', very warm and bright, and the loud voices of men could be heard distinctly. What a fool she had been to imagine that anything had happened to him! He was merely drinking over there at the 'Prince of Wales'. She faltered. She had never yet been to fetch him, and she never would go. So she continued her walk towards the long straggling line of houses, standing blank on the highway. She entered a passage between the dwellings.

"Mr Rigley?--Yes! Did you want him? No, he's not in at this minute."

The raw-boned woman leaned forward from her dark scullery and peered at the other, upon whom fell a dim light through the blind of the kitchen window.

"Is it Mrs Bates?" she asked in a tone tinged with respect.

"Yes. I wondered if your Master was at home. Mine hasn't come yet."

"'Asn't 'e! Oh, Jack's been 'ome an 'ad 'is dinner an' gone out. E's just gone for 'alf an hour afore bedtime. Did you call at the 'Prince of Wales'?"

"No--"

"No, you didn't like--! It's not very nice." The other woman was indulgent. There was an awkward pause. "Jack never said nothink about--about your Mester," she said.

"No!--I expect he's stuck in there!"

Elizabeth Bates said this bitterly, and with recklessness. She knew that the woman across the yard was standing at her door listening, but she did not care. As she turned:

"Stop a minute! I'll just go an' ask Jack if e' knows anythink," said Mrs Rigley.

"Oh, no--I wouldn't like to put--!"

"Yes, I will, if you'll just step inside an' see as th' childer doesn't come downstairs and set theirselves afire."

Elizabeth Bates, murmuring a remonstrance, stepped inside. The other woman apologized for the state of the room.

The kitchen needed apology. There were little frocks and trousers and childish undergarments on the squab and on the floor, and a litter of playthings everywhere. On the black American cloth of the table were pieces of bread and cake, crusts, slops, and a teapot with cold tea.

"Eh, ours is just as bad," said Elizabeth Bates, looking at the woman, not at the house. Mrs Rigley put a shawl over her head and hurried out, saying:

"I shanna be a minute."

The other sat, noting with faint disapproval the general untidiness of the room. Then she fell to counting the shoes of various sizes scattered over the floor. There were twelve. She sighed and said to herself, "No wonder!"--glancing at the litter. There came the scratching of two pairs of feet on the yard, and the Rigleys entered. Elizabeth Bates rose. Rigley was a big man, with very large bones. His head looked particularly bony. Across his temple was a blue scar, caused by a wound got in the pit, a wound in which the coal-dust remained blue like tattooing.

"Asna 'e come whoam yit?" asked the man, without any form of greeting, but with deference and sympathy. "I couldna say wheer he is--'e's non ower theer!"--he jerked his head to signify the 'Prince of Wales'.

"'E's 'appen gone up to th' 'Yew'," said Mrs Rigley.

There was another pause. Rigley had evidently something to get off his mind:

"Ah left 'im finishin' a stint," he began. "Loose-all 'ad bin gone about ten minutes when we com'n away, an' I shouted, 'Are ter comin', Walt?' an' 'e said, 'Go on, Ah shanna be but a'ef a minnit,' so we com'n ter th' bottom, me an' Bowers, thinkin' as 'e wor just behint, an' 'ud come up i' th' next bantle--"

He stood perplexed, as if answering a charge of deserting his mate. Elizabeth Bates, now again certain of disaster, hastened to reassure him:

"I expect 'e's gone up to th' 'Yew Tree', as you say. It's not the first time. I've fretted myself into a fever before now. He'll come home when they carry him."

"Ay, isn't it too bad!" deplored the other woman.

"I'll just step up to Dick's an' see if 'e IS theer," offered the man, afraid of appearing alarmed, afraid of taking liberties.

"Oh, I wouldn't think of bothering you that far," said Elizabeth Bates, with emphasis, but he knew she was glad of his offer.

As they stumbled up the entry, Elizabeth Bates heard Rigley's wife run across the yard and open her neighbour's door. At this, suddenly all the blood in her body seemed to switch away from her heart.

"Mind!" warned Rigley. "Ah've said many a time as Ah'd fill up them ruts in this entry, sumb'dy 'll be breakin' their legs yit."

She recovered herself and walked quickly along with the miner.

"I don't like leaving the children in bed, and nobody in the house," she said.

"No, you dunna!" he replied courteously. They were soon at the gate of the cottage.

"Well, I shanna be many minnits. Dunna you be frettin' now, 'e'll be all right," said the butty.

"Thank you very much, Mr Rigley," she replied.

"You're welcome!" he stammered, moving away. "I shanna be many minnits."

The house was quiet. Elizabeth Bates took off her hat and shawl, and rolled back the rug. When she had finished, she sat down. It was a few minutes past nine. She was startled by the rapid chuff of the winding-engine at the pit, and the sharp whirr of the brakes on the rope as it descended. Again she felt the painful sweep of her blood, and she put her hand to her side, saying aloud, "Good gracious!--it's only the nine o'clock deputy going down," rebuking herself.

She sat still, listening. Half an hour of this, and she was wearied out.

"What am I working myself up like this for?" she said pitiably to herself, "I s'll only be doing myself some damage."

She took out her sewing again.

At a quarter to ten there were footsteps. One person! She watched for the door to open. It was an elderly woman, in a black bonnet and a black woollen shawl--his mother. She was about sixty years old, pale, with blue eyes, and her face all wrinkled and lamentable. She shut the door and turned to her daughter-inlaw peevishly.

"Eh, Lizzie, whatever shall we do, whatever shall we do!" she cried.

Elizabeth drew back a little, sharply.

"What is it, mother?" she said.

The elder woman seated herself on the sofa.

"I don't know, child, I can't tell you!"--she shook her head slowly. Elizabeth sat watching her, anxious and vexed.

"I don't know," replied the grandmother, sighing very deeply. "There's no end to my troubles, there isn't. The things I've gone through, I'm sure it's enough--!" She wept without wiping her eyes, the tears running.

"But, mother," interrupted Elizabeth, "what do you mean? What is it?"

The grandmother slowly wiped her eyes. The fountains of her tears were stopped by Elizabeth's directness. She wiped her eyes slowly.

"Poor child! Eh, you poor thing!" she moaned. "I don't know what we're going to do, I don't--and you as you are--it's a thing, it is indeed!"

Elizabeth waited.

"Is he dead?" she asked, and at the words her heart swung violently, though she felt a slight flush of shame at the ultimate extravagance of the question. Her words sufficiently frightened the old lady, almost brought her to herself.

"Don't say so, Elizabeth! We'll hope it's not as bad as that; no, may the Lord spare us that, Elizabeth. Jack Rigley came just as I was sittin' down to a glass afore going to bed, an' 'e said, "Appen you'll go down th' line, Mrs Bates. Walt's had an accident. 'Appen you'll go an' sit wi' 'er till we can get him home.' I hadn't time to ask him a word afore he was gone. An' I put my bonnet on an' come straight down, Lizzie. I thought to myself, 'Eh, that poor blessed child, if anybody should come an' tell her of a sudden, there's no knowin' what'll 'appen to 'er.' You mustn't let it upset you, Lizzie--or you know what to expect. How long is it, six months--or is it five, Lizzie? Ay!"-- the old woman shook her head--"time slips on, it slips on! Ay!"

Elizabeth's thoughts were busy elsewhere. If he was killed--would she be able to manage on the little pension and what she could earn?--she counted up rapidly. If he was hurt--they wouldn't take him to the hospital-- how tiresome he would be to nurse!--but perhaps she'd be able to get him away from the drink and his hateful ways. She would--while he was ill. The tears offered to come to her eyes at the picture. But what sentimental luxury was this she was beginning?--She turned to consider the children. At any rate she was absolutely necessary for them. They were her business.

"Ay!" repeated the old woman, "it seems but a week or two since he brought me his first wages. Ay--he was a good lad, Elizabeth, he was, in his way. I don't know why he got to be such a trouble, I don't. He was a happy lad at home, only full of spirits. But there's no mistake he's been a handful of trouble, he has! I hope the Lord'll spare him to mend his ways. I hope so, I hope so. You've had a sight o' trouble with him, Elizabeth, you have indeed. But he was a jolly enough lad wi' me, he was, I can assure you. I don't know how it is . . ."

The old woman continued to muse aloud, a monotonous irritating sound, while Elizabeth thought concentratedly, startled once, when she heard the winding-engine chuff quickly, and the brakes skirr with a shriek. Then she heard the engine more slowly, and the brakes made no sound. The old woman did not notice. Elizabeth waited in suspense. The mother-inlaw talked, with lapses into silence.

"But he wasn't your son, Lizzie, an' it makes a difference. Whatever he was, I remember him when he was little, an' I learned to understand him and to make allowances. You've got to make allowances for them--"

It was half-past ten, and the old woman was saying: "But it's trouble from beginning to end; you're never too old for trouble, never too old for that--" when the gate banged back, and there were heavy feet on the steps.

"I'll go, Lizzie, let me go," cried the old woman, rising. But Elizabeth was at the door. It was a man in pit-clothes.

"They're bringin' 'im, Missis," he said. Elizabeth's heart halted a moment. Then it surged on again, almost suffocating her.

"Is he--is it bad?" she asked.

The man turned away, looking at the darkness:

"The doctor says 'e'd been dead hours. 'E saw 'im i' th' lamp-cabin."

The old woman, who stood just behind Elizabeth, dropped into a chair, and folded her hands, crying: "Oh, my boy, my boy!"

"Hush!" said Elizabeth, with a sharp twitch of a frown. "Be still, mother, don't waken th' children: I wouldn't have them down for anything!"

The old woman moaned softly, rocking herself. The man was drawing away. Elizabeth took a step forward.

"How was it?" she asked.

"Well, I couldn't say for sure," the man replied, very ill at ease. "'E wor finishin' a stint an' th' butties 'ad gone, an' a lot o' stuff come down atop 'n 'im."

"And crushed him?" cried the widow, with a shudder.

"No," said the man, "it fell at th' back of 'im. 'E wor under th' face, an' it niver touched 'im. It shut 'im in. It seems 'e wor smothered."

Elizabeth shrank back. She heard the old woman behind her cry:

"What?--what did 'e say it was?"

The man replied, more loudly: "'E wor smothered!"

Then the old woman wailed aloud, and this relieved Elizabeth.

"Oh, mother," she said, putting her hand on the old woman, "don't waken th' children, don't waken th' children."

She wept a little, unknowing, while the old mother rocked herself and moaned. Elizabeth remembered that they were bringing him home, and she must be ready. "They'll lay him in the parlour," she said to herself, standing a moment pale and perplexed.

Then she lighted a candle and went into the tiny room. The air was cold and damp, but she could not make a fire, there was no fireplace. She set down the candle and looked round. The candle-light glittered on the lustre-glasses, on the two vases that held some of the pink chrysanthemums, and on the dark mahogany. There was a cold, deathly smell of chrysanthemums in the room. Elizabeth stood looking at the flowers. She turned away, and calculated whether there would be room to lay him on the floor, between the couch and the chiffonier. She pushed the chairs aside. There would be room to lay him down and to step round him. Then she fetched the old red tablecloth, and another old cloth, spreading them down to save her bit of carpet. She shivered on leaving the parlour; so, from the dresser-drawer she took a clean shirt and put it at the fire to air. All the time her mother-inlaw was rocking herself in the chair and moaning.

"You'll have to move from there, mother," said Elizabeth. "They'll be bringing him in. Come in the rocker."

The old mother rose mechanically, and seated herself by the fire, continuing to lament. Elizabeth went into the pantry for another candle, and there, in the little penthouse under the naked tiles, she heard them coming. She stood still in the pantry doorway, listening. She heard them pass the end of the house, and come awkwardly down the three steps, a jumble of shuffling footsteps and muttering voices. The old woman was silent. The men were in the yard.

Then Elizabeth heard Matthews, the manager of the pit, say: "You go in first, Jim. Mind!"

The door came open, and the two women saw a collier backing into the room, holding one end of a stretcher, on which they could see the nailed pit-boots of the dead man. The two carriers halted, the man at the head stooping to the lintel of the door.

"Wheer will you have him?" asked the manager, a short, white-bearded man.

Elizabeth roused herself and came from the pantry carrying the unlighted candle.

"In the parlour," she said.

"In there, Jim!" pointed the manager, and the carriers backed round into the tiny room. The coat with which they had covered the body fell off as they awkwardly turned through the two doorways, and the women saw their man, naked to the waist, lying stripped for work. The old woman began to moan in a low voice of horror.

"Lay th' stretcher at th' side," snapped the manager, "an' put 'im on th' cloths. Mind now, mind! Look you now--!"

One of the men had knocked off a vase of chrysanthemums. He stared awkwardly, then they set down the stretcher. Elizabeth did not look at her husband. As soon as she could get in the room, she went and picked up the broken vase and the flowers.

"Wait a minute!" she said.

The three men waited in silence while she mopped up the water with a duster.

"Eh, what a job, what a job, to be sure!" the manager was saying, rubbing his brow with trouble and perplexity. "Never knew such a thing in my life, never! He'd no business to ha' been left. I never knew such a thing in my life! Fell over him clean as a whistle, an' shut him in. Not four foot of space, there wasn't--yet it scarce bruised him."

He looked down at the dead man, lying prone, half naked, all grimed with coal-dust.

""Sphyxiated,' the doctor said. It IS the most terrible job I've ever known. Seems as if it was done o' purpose. Clean over him, an' shut 'im in, like a mouse-trap"--he made a sharp, descending gesture with his hand.

The colliers standing by jerked aside their heads in hopeless comment.

The horror of the thing bristled upon them all.

Then they heard the girl's voice upstairs calling shrilly: "Mother, mother--who is it? Mother, who is it?"

Elizabeth hurried to the foot of the stairs and opened the door:

"Go to sleep!" she commanded sharply. "What are you shouting about? Go to sleep at once--there's nothing--"

Then she began to mount the stairs. They could hear her on the boards, and on the plaster floor of the little bedroom. They could hear her distinctly:

"What's the matter now?--what's the matter with you, silly thing?"--her voice was much agitated, with an unreal gentleness.

"I thought it was some men come," said the plaintive voice of the child. "Has he come?"

"Yes, they've brought him. There's nothing to make a fuss about. Go to sleep now, like a good child."

They could hear her voice in the bedroom, they waited whilst she covered the children under the bedclothes.

"Is he drunk?" asked the girl, timidly, faintly.

"No! No--he's not! He--he's asleep."

"Is he asleep downstairs?"

"Yes--and don't make a noise."

There was silence for a moment, then the men heard the frightened child again:

"What's that noise?"

"It's nothing, I tell you, what are you bothering for?"

The noise was the grandmother moaning. She was oblivious of everything, sitting on her chair rocking and moaning. The manager put his hand on her arm and bade her "Sh--sh!!"

The old woman opened her eyes and looked at him. She was shocked by this interruption, and seemed to wonder.

"What time is it?"--the plaintive thin voice of the child, sinking back unhappily into sleep, asked this last question.

"Ten o'clock," answered the mother more softly. Then she must have bent down and kissed the children.

Matthews beckoned to the men to come away. They put on their caps and took up the stretcher. Stepping over the body, they tiptoed out of the house. None of them spoke till they were far from the wakeful children.

When Elizabeth came down she found her mother alone on the parlour floor, leaning over the dead man, the tears dropping on him.

"We must lay him out," the wife said. She put on the kettle, then returning knelt at the feet, and began to unfasten the knotted leather laces. The room was clammy and dim with only one candle, so that she had to bend her face almost to the floor. At last she got off the heavy boots and put them away.

"You must help me now," she whispered to the old woman. Together they stripped the man.

When they arose, saw him lying in the naive dignity of death, the women stood arrested in fear and respect. For a few moments they remained still, looking down, the old mother whimpering. Elizabeth felt countermanded.

She saw him, how utterly inviolable he lay in himself. She had nothing to do with him. She could not accept it. Stooping, she laid her hand on him, in claim. He was still warm, for the mine was hot where he had died. His mother had his face between her hands, and was murmuring incoherently. The old tears fell in succession as drops from wet leaves; the mother was not weeping, merely her tears flowed. Elizabeth embraced the body of her husband, with cheek and lips. She seemed to be listening, inquiring, trying to get some connection. But she could not. She was driven away. He was impregnable.

She rose, went into the kitchen, where she poured warm water into a bowl, brought soap and flannel and a soft towel.

"I must wash him," she said.

Then the old mother rose stiffly, and watched Elizabeth as she carefully washed his face, carefully brushing the big blond moustache from his mouth with the flannel. She was afraid with a bottomless fear, so she ministered to him. The old woman, jealous, said:

"Let me wipe him!"--and she kneeled on the other side drying slowly as Elizabeth washed, her big black bonnet sometimes brushing the dark head of her daughter. They worked thus in silence for a long time. They never forgot it was death, and the touch of the man's dead body gave them strange emotions, different in each of the women; a great dread possessed them both, the mother felt the lie was given to her womb, she was denied; the wife felt the utter isolation of the human soul, the child within her was a weight apart from her.

At last it was finished. He was a man of handsome body, and his face showed no traces of drink. He was blonde, full-fleshed, with fine limbs. But he was dead.

"Bless him," whispered his mother, looking always at his face, and speaking out of sheer terror. "Dear lad--bless him!" She spoke in a faint, sibilant ecstasy of fear and mother love.

Elizabeth sank down again to the floor, and put her face against his neck, and trembled and shuddered. But she had to draw away again. He was dead, and her living flesh had no place against his. A great dread and weariness held her: she was so unavailing. Her life was gone like this.

"White as milk he is, clear as a twelve-month baby, bless him, the darling!" the old mother murmured to herself. "Not a mark on him, clear and clean and white, beautiful as ever a child was made," she murmured with pride. Elizabeth kept her face hidden.

"He went peaceful, Lizzie--peaceful as sleep. Isn't he beautiful, the lamb? Ay--he must ha' made his peace, Lizzie. 'Appen he made it all right, Lizzie, shut in there. He'd have time. He wouldn't look like this if he hadn't made his peace. The lamb, the dear lamb. Eh, but he had a hearty laugh. I loved to hear it. He had the heartiest laugh, Lizzie, as a lad--"

Elizabeth looked up. The man's mouth was fallen back, slightly open under the cover of the moustache. The eyes, half shut, did not show glazed in the obscurity. Life with its smoky burning gone from him, had left him apart and utterly alien to her. And she knew what a stranger he was to her. In her womb was ice of fear, because of this separate stranger with whom she had been living as one flesh. Was this what it all meant--utter, intact separateness, obscured by heat of living? In dread she turned her face away. The fact was too deadly. There had been nothing between them, and yet they had come together, exchanging their nakedness repeatedly. Each time he had taken her, they had been two isolated beings, far apart as now. He was no more responsible than she. The child was like ice in her womb. For as she looked at the dead man, her mind, cold and detached, said clearly: "Who am I? What have I been doing? I have been fighting a husband who did not exist. *He* existed all the time. What wrong have I done? What was that I have been living with? There lies the reality, this man."--And her soul died in her for fear: she knew she had never seen him, he had never seen her, they had met in the dark and had fought in the dark, not knowing whom they met nor whom they fought. And now she saw, and turned silent in seeing. For she had been wrong. She had said he was something he was not; she had felt familiar with him. Whereas he was apart all the while, living as she never lived, feeling as she never felt.

In fear and shame she looked at his naked body, that she had known falsely. And he was the father of her children. Her soul was torn from her body and stood apart. She looked at his naked body and was ashamed, as if she had denied it. After all, it was itself. It seemed awful to her. She looked at his face, and she turned her own face to the wall. For his look was other than hers, his way was not her way. She had denied him what he was--she saw it now. She had refused him as himself.--And this had been her life, and his life.--She was grateful to death, which restored the truth. And she knew she was not dead.

And all the while her heart was bursting with grief and pity for him. What had he suffered? What stretch of horror for this helpless man! She was rigid with agony. She had not been able to help him. He had been cruelly injured, this naked man, this other being, and she could make no reparation. There were the children--but the children belonged to life. This dead man had nothing to do with them. He and she were only channels through which life had flowed to issue in the children. She was a mother-- but how awful she knew it now to have been a wife. And he, dead now, how awful he must have felt it to be a husband. She felt that in the next world he would be a stranger to her. If they met there, in the beyond, they would only be ashamed of what had been before. The children had come, for some mysterious reason, out of both of them. But the children did not unite them. Now he was dead, she knew how eternally he was apart from her, how eternally he had nothing more to do with her. She saw this episode of her life closed. They had denied each other in life. Now he had withdrawn. An anguish came over her. It was finished then: it had become hopeless between them long before he died. Yet he had been her husband. But how little!--

"Have you got his shirt, 'Lizabeth?"

Elizabeth turned without answering, though she strove to weep and behave as her mother-inlaw expected. But she could not, she was silenced. She went into the kitchen and returned with the garment.

"It is aired," she said, grasping the cotton shirt here and there to try. She was almost ashamed to handle him; what right had she or anyone to lay hands on him; but her touch was humble on his body. It was hard work to clothe him. He was so heavy and inert. A terrible dread gripped her all the while: that he could be so heavy and utterly inert, unresponsive, apart. The horror of the distance between them was almost too much for her--it was so infinite a gap she must look across.

At last it was finished. They covered him with a sheet and left him lying, with his face bound. And she fastened the door of the little parlour, lest the children should see what was lying there. Then, with peace sunk heavy on her heart, she went about making tidy the kitchen. She knew she submitted to life, which was her immediate master. But from death, her ultimate master, she winced with fear and shame.

Analysis

Author

David Herbert Lawrence (1885 – 1930) is better known as a novelist. He was born in the coal-mining town of Eastwood near Nottingham and came from a working class background – his father was a coal miner. Lawrence's mother came from a slightly higher class and was unhappy in her marriage to a drunken, feckless miner. Some of Lawrence's fiction – and 'Odour of Chrysanthemums' falls into this category – features a domineering wife with social aspirations, unhappily married to a boorish, loutish working class man.

In adult life, especially after the First World War, Lawrence travelled widely, wrote some acclaimed travel books, and also wrote over 800 poems, most of them in free verse. He also wrote some well-known short stories and several plays. Lawrence believed in spontaneity and naturalness, and many of his poems are about love and relationships: indeed, some of his novels were banned in his lifetime for obscenity. He felt that modern man was insulated by technology and civilization from his true self and from nature. As time has gone on, he is increasingly admired for his short stories and his unflinching yet empathetic portrayal of English working class life – as in 'Odour of Chrysanthemums'. His novels brought him notoriety during his lifetime, but many readers would agree that he is a master of the short story form.

Context

Lawrence wrote the story in 1909 and it was first published in 'The English Review' in July 1911. It was then published in book form in 'The Prussian Officer and Other Stories' on 26th November 1914. Lawrence later turned the story into a play entitled 'The Widowing of Mrs Holroyd'. When Lawrence wrote the story Great Britain was the world's superpower and its Empire covered over a third of the world. Apart from voyages of discovery and exploration, the driving force behind Britain's pre-eminence had been the Industrial Revolution. From an economic point of view the Industrial Revolution had made the country very wealthy, but it was not such good news for the working classes, forced to work long hours in sometimes dangerous and hazardous conditions. In particular, working conditions for Britain's miners were appalling, and they faced frequent death from suffocation, being crushed by cave-ins and through explosions of underground gas. But coal was necessary to keep the factories supplied with energy; at its height more than a million and a half men worked as coal miners. Lawrence draws carefully on his own experience of working class life which helps give the story an authentic aura. The Industrial Revolution had a huge demographic impact: in 1780 most of the population of Britain lived in the countryside and worked the land; by the time Lawrence is writing most of the population lived in industrial cities or towns and were employed in factories or mines. Although Lawrence's father never died in a mining accident, he is writing about a community he knew well.

During the period that this story was written and then published two important social movements were occurring: the suffragette movement which was campaigning to get women the vote and to revolutionize male/female relationships; and the labour movement which through the trades unions and the newly formed Labour Party sought to improve the lives of the working class. Lawrence has no interest in this story on dealing with these movements at all, preferring to present the problems of Walter and Elizabeth Bates as a more elemental clash of the sexes and of different personalities.

Unfamiliar Words

What follows is a list of formal words of which you may not know the meaning, slang terms used by the mining community in Nottinghamshire, and phonetic spelling of the characters' speech which adds realistic detail.

spinney – a small clump of trees

whimsey – a pit pool formed by any water brought to the surface along with the coal.

pit-bank – a huge mound of earth, rock, coal dust and small pieces of coal, brought to the surface and discarded as unusable rubbish.

sidings – several parallel rows of railway tracks which lead nowhere and are used to 'park' railway engines or wagons that are not in use.

the two wheels… the winding engine – the winding engine is the mechanism that brings cages of miners up to the surface and down to work. Around the two wheels there would have been a thick rope or chain to operate the lift machinery.

winter-crack trees – a type of plum tree with late-ripening plums.

imperious – domineering and powerful.

mien – a look or bearing.

taciturn – silent or not talkative.

wan – pale.

mash – to brew a pot of tea

censure – blame or unfavourable judgment.

Walter's got another bout on – Walter intends to go on a drinking spree.

heered - heard

The Lord Nelson – a local pub.

to spend that b------ afore he went – to spend that bugger (presumably a sum of money) before he left the pub.

A' Saturday night – on Saturday night

It's a settler, it is – Elizabeth's father is praising the tea for settling his stomach.

pertinacity – the quality of being obstinate and stubborn.

Her child chid her… - 'chid' is the past tense of 'to chide; although we would now use 'chided'. If you chide someone you tell them off mildly.

The Prince of Wales – another local pub.

ripping – looking through the pit-bank for small pieces of coal to use on the fire at home.

wafflin' it – waving the piece of bread around aimlessly in front of the fire.

crozzled up – burnt up and singed.

I canna see – I cannot see.

wrath – anger.

sleepers – the huge blocks of wood that railway tracks are laid on.

plaintively – mournfully.

stile – a step for climbing over a wall or fence.

scullery – a room for kitchen work which here doubles as the kitchen itself.

Master – husband.

Mester – phonetic spelling of 'Master'.

childer – dialect word for children.

remonstrance – a strong protest.

I shanna be a minute – I won't be a minute.

Asna 'e come whoam yet? – Hasn't he come home yet?

E's 'appen gone up to th' 'Yew' – The Yew is another local pub.

Ah left him finishing a stint – I left him finishing a piece of work.

Loose-all – the signal for the men to finish work.

Are ter comin', Walt? An' 'e said, 'Go on, Ah shanna be but a 'ef minnit,' so we com'n ter th' bottom, me and Bowers. Thinkin' as 'e wor just behint, an' ''ud come up in the next bantle – Are you coming, Walter? And he said. 'Go on, I won't be half a minute so Bowers and I arrived at the lift. We thought we was just behind us and would come up in the next batch.

Mind!.... Ah've said many a time as Ah'd fill up them ruts in this entry, sumb'dy'll be breaking their legs yit – Be careful! I said many times I would fill up the ruts in this entrance yard or someone will break their legs one day.

I shanna be many minnits. Dunna you be frettin' now' 'e'll be all right – I won't be long. Don't you worry now – he'll be all right.

butty – workmate.

rebuking herself – telling herself off.

peevishly – fretfully and with worry.

vexed – annoyed and troubled.

You mustn't let this upset you, or you know what to expect. How long is it, six months – or is it five? – Elizabeth's mother-in-law is advising her to remain calm or the shock of Walter's accident may bring on a miscarriage and she might lose the baby she is carrying.

"E wor finishing a stint an' th' butties 'ad gone an' a lot o' stuff come down upon him – He was finishing a piece of work and his work-mates had gone and the roof caved in.

… it fell at th' back of him. 'E wor under th' face, an' it never touched 'im. It shut him in. It seems he wor smothered – The cave-in was behind him, so he was not crushed. He was by the coal face and was untouched by the cave-in. But because the cave-in shut him in, he had a limited supply of oxygen and suffocated.

parlour – what we would now call the front room or living room. Used in the past only for very special or out-of-the-ordinary situations.

chiffonier – an ornamental cabinet.

collier – a coal miner.

perplexity – confusion or embarrassment.

'Sphyxiated – asphyxiated, suffocated for want of air to breathe.

countermanded – 'to countermand' literally means to cancel or over-turn an order; here it seems that the sight of Walter's dead body has cancelled all her previous feelings about his death.

inviolable – something that can no longer be hurt or distressed.

impregnable – something that cannot be attacked or threatened.

sibilant – hissing.

reparation – to make compensation or amends for some wrong that has occurred.

Plot

The story is written in the third person but is told exclusively from the point of view of Elizabeth Bates, the wife of a miner and mother to John and Annie. She is pregnant with the couple's third child. The story begins with a railway engine pulling seven wagons full of coal. Lawrence is intent in this opening paragraph on presenting the gloomy environment of the pit village and to show the effect of heavy mining on the area. It is dusk and autumn – 'the withered oak leaves dropped noiselessly' – and the railway engine startles a colt while causing a woman to stop walking until the train has passed: she 'stood insignificantly trapped between the jolting black wagons and the hedge'. Lawrence is describing the scene realistically, but he is also using pathetic fallacy: this is going to be a gloomy story and one that revolves around the coal mine. In a long description Lawrence shows how the coal pit has blighted the landscape:

The fields were dreary and forsaken, and in the marshy strip that led to the whimsey, a reedy pit-pond, the fowls had already abandoned their run among the alders, to roost in the tiled fowl-house. The pit-bank loomed up beyond the pond, flames like red sores licking its ashy sides, in the afternoon's stagnant light.

The wheels on the two headstocks are moving, bringing the miners up to the ground at the end of the working day. In the photo above (which is of a Nottinghamshire pit) you can clearly see the winding wheels and the head stocks which support them. The winding wheels operate the lift machinery, bringing cages of miners to the surface. Also on the right of the photo is the pit-bank where coal dust, earth and unusable fragments of coal were piled and any other detritus that was brought to the surface in the process of extracting the coal. Lawrence's description of its 'red sores licking its ashes sides' personifies it and makes it sound thoroughly evil.

Miners start to appear walking to their homes and Lawrence turns the reader's attention to a 'low cottage' and Elizabeth Bates, who is calling her son in because it is getting dark. John, aged 5, has been lurking among the raspberry canes. He is clearly reluctant to come in and as he and his mother walk towards the house 'he tore at the ragged wisps of chrysanthemums and dropped the petals in handfuls along the path' – for which his mother reprimands him, saying it looks 'nasty'. On impulse she picks a sprig of the flowers and places them in her apron band.

At this point a railway engine pulls up opposite the gate of the house: it is being driven by Elizabeth's father. She takes him a cup of tea and a piece of bread and butter. Elizabeth's father is obviously a widower and tells her rather defensively that he plans to re-marry in order not to be alone as he reaches old age. He is defensive, it seems, because he has not been a widower for long – it is not long since Elizabeth's mother died. He also brings news that Elizabeth's husband, Walter, has been bragging about going on a drinking spree and boasting openly about how much money he will spend in the pub.

Her father drives on and Elizabeth returns to the house, where the table is set for tea. Annie, her daughter, enters and is rebuked mildly by Elizabeth for being late home from school – it now being dark outside. Elizabeth asks Annie if she has seen her father, but she hasn't. At Annie's urging they start the meal without Walter, but Elizabeth eats little and is clearly preoccupied with the thought that her husband is in the pub spending money and not with his family. She listens to the colliery winding gear, but it is silent and consoles herself with the thought that he may have stopped to do some 'ripping' – searching through the slag heap to find usable pieces of coal.

Elizabeth puts more coal on the fire which makes the room darker and John complains, so Elizabeth lights the central oil lamp. Lawrence uses her action in doing so to reveal that she is pregnant and it also allows Annie to see the sprig of chrysanthemums in her mother's apron band at which she expresses surprise and delight: '"You've got a flower in your apron!" said the child at this unusual event.'

But Elizabeth does not share her daughter's enthusiasm and disagrees that they smell beautiful (in an important quotation we will return to later):

"'No.' she said, *'not to me. It was chrysanthemums when I married him, and chrysanthemums when you were born, and the first time they ever brought him home drunk, he'd got brown chrysanthemums in his button-hole.'"*

As the meal comes to an end, Mrs Bates gives full vent to her anger at her husband:

"'Twenty minutes to six!' In a tone of bitter carelessness she continued: *'Eh, he'll not come home till they bring him. There he'll stick! But he needn't come rolling in here in his pit-dirt, for I won't wash him. He can lie on the floor – Eh, what a fool I've been, what a fool! And this is what I came here for, to this dirty hole, rats and all, for him to slink past his very door. Twice last week….'*

The children play quietly for an hour 'united in fear of their mother's wrath, and in dread of their father's home-coming', while the mother sews keeping her ears open for anyone walking outside.
Then it is time for bed: the children wash and say their prayers, and Elizabeth Bates takes up her sewing again but now – in a foreshadowing of what is to come – '…her anger was tinged with fear.'

Chapter Two of the story begins at eight o'clock that same evening. Elizabeth leaves the house and the children sleeping to find her husband. As she walks to a neighbour's house she berates herself for imagining that 'anything had happened to him'. She calls on Mrs Rigley whose husband has been home for his meal, but has gone briefly to the pub. Mrs Rigley offers to help and fetches her husband from the pub. He says that the last he saw of Walter was in the coal mine finishing a job at the coal face. Mr Rigley kindly offers to check in the other pubs for Walter and walks Mrs Bates home before departing on his errand.

Elizabeth Bates waits for another forty-five minutes when her mother-in-law bursts into the house because she has heard Walter has had an accident in the pit. Elizabeth tries to calm and quieten her, so the children's sleep is not disturbed. A man arrives in pit clothes with the news that Walter is dead – suffocated because of a cave-in close to where he was working which briefly cut him off from the main mine. By the time the other miners had cleared the cave-in Walter had been asphyxiated. Walter's mother wails hysterically but Elizabeth acts calmly, clearing a space in the parlour and laying down a cloth for the body of her husband to be laid upon.

Quite soon the pit manager and a miner arrive with Walter's body on a stretcher. As they bring the body into the parlour they knock over a vase of chrysanthemums on the table, breaking the vase; Elizabeth quickly clears up the mess – typically for Elizabeth, keeping the home as neat and tidy as possible before cleaning her husband's dead body. The commotion downstairs has woken Annie and Elizabeth goes upstairs to quieten her and get her back to sleep, not mentioning Walter's death – that can wait until the morning.

When the men have left the house, Elizabeth and her mother-in-law start to wash and then clothe Walter's body. Lawrence presents Elizabeth reflecting on her marriage to Walter and finally coming to an understanding of it and why it was unsuccessful. Elizabeth even has an epiphany of sorts when she admits to herself that she was partly to blame for the failure of her marriage. This is discussed in greater length below when we consider Elizabeth's character.

Characters

Elizabeth Bates

Lawrence's first description of Elizabeth Bates neatly summarizes her appearance and her character:

She was a tall woman of imperious mien, handsome, with definite black eyebrows. Her smooth black hair was parted exactly.

For most of the story she is angry and bitter at the thought of her husband drinking precious money away in a local pub. Many of her speeches are delivered 'bitterly' and is described by Lawrence as 'bitter'. She seems to feel that she has thrown away all chance of happiness by marrying Walter and she says at one point:

Eh, what a fool I've been, what a fool! And this is what I came here for, to this dirty hole, rats and all, for him to slink past his very door.

When Annie admires the chrysanthemums tucked in her mother's waistband, Elizabeth calls her 'silly' and removes the flowers 'irritably', before going on to say, in response to Annie's saying that they smell 'beautiful':

No... not to me. It was chrysanthemums when I married him, and chrysanthemums when you were born, and the first time they ever brought him home drunk, he'd got brown chrysanthemums in his button-hole.

Chrysanthemums play an important role in the story which we examine later.

Elizabeth runs an orderly house and takes pride in the tidiness of the kitchen area. She ensures the children eat, have time to play after the meal, washes them before bed and ensures they say their prayers. However, from what we see in the story she is not very loving and maternal: while they play the children are subdued and do not want to incur their mother's wrath. Nor does she congratulate her father on hearing that he plans to re-marry. She is organized – like her exactly parted hair - but lacks a loving touch perhaps. However, when Walter's mother arrives and later when the mine workers bring Walter's body into the parlour, Elizabeth is very careful that the noise and commotion does not disturb the children's sleep. Annie does wake up when her father's corpse is put in the parlour but Elizabeth goes up to her and soothes her back to sleep in a gentle and motherly way.

Lawrence is careful to ensure that Elizabeth uses Standard English and not the local accent and she appears to see herself as superior to the rest of the community. For example, she will not demean herself by going into a pub to look for her husband, but is happy for Mrs Rigley to go to the pub to summon her husband; she also views the chaotic untidiness of the Rigley's kitchen with an air of superiority.

However, in the short period of the story when she and her mother-in-law know that Walter had had an accident, but don't know how bad it is, Elizabeth is entirely pragmatic, wondering if he is bed-ridden for a few weeks whether she can stop him drinking altogether, or trying to work out, if he is dead, whether she will be able to manage financially. Her main concern is the children; 'She turned to consider the children. At any rate she was absolutely necessary for them. They were her business.'

But Elizabeth is not devoid of emotion. When confirmation finally comes that Walter has died in the mine 'she wept a little, unknowing' and then remembered that 'they were bringing him home and she must be ready, so she goes and prepares the parlour: significantly there is the 'cold, deathly smell of chrysanthemums in the room'.

Elizabeth and her mother-in-law stand 'arrested in fear and respect' at the sight of Walter naked and they start to clean him. Lawrence writes;

She saw him, how utterly inviolable he lay in himself. She had nothing to do with him. She could not accept it. Stooping down, she laid her hand on him, in claim ....Elizabeth embraced the body of her husband, with cheek and lips. She seemed to be listening, inquiring, trying to get a connection. But she could not. She was driven away. He was impregnable.

Death is the final isolation that awaits us all. As she looks at Walter's body, Elizabeth reflects on her life with him and concludes that he was a stranger to her, just as she was a stranger to him:

There had been nothing between them, and yet they had come together, exchanging their nakedness repeatedly. Each time he had taken her, they had been two isolated beings, far apart as now. He was no more responsible than she.

She seems to accept some responsibility for the failure of their marriage or their unhappiness in it:

...she knew she had never seen him, he had never seen her, they had met in the dark and fought in the dark, not knowing whom they met or whom they fought. And now she saw and turned silent in seeing. For she had been wrong. She had said he was something he was not; she had felt familiar with him. Whereas he was apart all the while, feeling as she never felt.

Lawrence sums up this train of thought by writing "she had refused him as himself". Lawrence also presents Elizabeth as capable of intense emotion and empathy at the close of the story:

... her heart was bursting with grief and pity for him. What had he suffered? What stretch of horror for this helpless man! She was rigid with agony. She had not been able to help him. He had been cruelly injured, this naked man, this other being, and she could make no reparation.

She acknowledges that the children had not helped bring them closer together and, if they were to meet in an after-life, they would be strangers to each other. She ruefully thinks 'how awful' it had been to be a wife, but also recognizes 'how awful he must have felt it to be a husband'. Elizabeth feels 'a terrible dread' and Lawrence writes that 'the horror of the distance between them was almost too much for her' – the distance between life and death, especially given their physical intimacy in life as man and wife.

Lawrence ends the story on a harsh and sombre note:

She knew she submitted to life, which was her immediate master. But from death, her ultimate master, she winced with fear.

Annie Bates

Annie is the seven-year-old daughter of Walter and Elizabeth Bates and is already at school. Lawrence presents her as less self-centred than her brother. She understands why her mother is angry with Walter for going to the pub – she is capable of emotional empathy without once expressing antagonism towards her father. She is old enough to understand that a prolonged bout in the pub by Walter will lead to marital discord.

She is different from her mother, however: she enthuses about the sprig of chrysanthemums that her mother has placed in her apron – an enthusiastic response because it is clear that Elizabeth rarely does such things and she dismisses Annie's rapture over the flowers as 'silly'. While toasting the bread in front of the fire she imaginatively says, "I do think it's beautiful to look in the fire…. It's so red and full of little caves – and it feels so nice and you can fair smell it". Her reaction to the flowers and to the fire show that Annie possesses an enthusiasm for life that her mother has lost.

Annie is woken by the men taking Walter's body into the parlour and shouts down to her mother. Perhaps she has been awake all this time, waiting for her father's arrival – since she understands the implications for family harmony if he rolls back drunk. Elizabeth soothingly placates her and tells her that her father is asleep downstairs. News of the death can wait until the morning.

John Bates

John is the five-year-old son of Walter and Elizabeth Bates. At the start of the story Elizabeth is looking for him, worried that he is near the brook at the bottom of the garden, but, in fact, he is hiding among the raspberry canes. He wears a man's clothes that have been cut down so that they will fit him. Lawrence describes him as 'taciturn' and Elizabeth Bates sees both herself and her husband in her son as he whittles a piece of wood with a knife:

As the mother watched her son's sullen little struggle with the wood, she saw herself in his silence and pertinacity; she saw the father in her child's indifference to all but himself.

In the whole story John remains sullen, speaking only to tell his mother where he is at the start and to complain about the way Annie is toasting the bread before the fire. When the children say their prayers at bedtime, it is typical of John that he mumbles his.

Walter Bates

Although the reader never sees Walter alive in the story, in some ways he is the central character because almost everything in the story revolves around him. Walter is not an alcoholic – alcoholics cannot go for a single day without alcohol – but instead Walter goes on periodic drinking sprees on which he drinks himself into a stupor and has to be carried home – as Elizabeth predicts will happen this evening. From what others say – Elizabeth, Elizabeth's father, Walter's mother – we get the impression that Walter is a feckless, irresponsible drunkard who prefers the pub to the company of his wife and children. However, Walter is not a lazy man – Mr Rigley says Walter stayed at work after the signal to stop work had been given – and working in a coal mine (as Walter's death shows) was an extremely hazardous job: injuries and deaths were common events. We can only guess that Walter's drinking bouts were a reaction to working every day in the pit. When his dead body is brought home, he is naked, innocent and vulnerable, and the sight of him allows Elizabeth to reach a more balanced, more sympathetic view of their marriage acknowledging her role in its failure.

We also learn that Walter was good-looking man, with strong limbs and a moustache. Elizabeth must have been attracted to something in him in order to have married him in the first place, and she is pregnant with their third child, so the marriage was not completely dead.

Walter's Mother

Elizabeth Bates's mother-in-law arrives with the news that Walter has had an accident down the pit. Lawrence uses the mother-in-law in two clear ways: firstly, she is used to build tension because we know that Walter has had an accident but not that he is dead – that news comes later; secondly, Lawrence uses her almost hysterical reaction as a contrast to Elizabeth's more practical and calm approach – Elizabeth is upset and shocked, but not so overt in her emotions. Ever practical, she is already thinking that if Walter is injured and in bed, it will be a good opportunity to wean him from alcohol, and, if he is dead, whether she will be able to manage financially – with a pension from the coal company and her own earnings. The mother-in-law's extrovert weeping and wailing is in clear contrast to Elizabeth's calm and stoical response.

Of course, Walter's mother has known him all his life and can remember him as a child. So she is slightly more indulgent towards his behaviour as an adult. She says:

Ay – he was a good lad, Elizabeth, he was, in his way. I don't know why he got to be such a trouble, I don't. He was a happy lad at home, only full of spirits. But there's no mistake he's been a handful of trouble, he has! ….You've had a sight of trouble with him, Elizabeth, you have indeed.

Even his own mother recognizes Walter's irresponsible behaviour with money and alcohol.

Mrs Rigley

Mrs Rigley is a neighbour who Elizabeth approaches for help in discovering Walter's whereabouts. She has six children – there are twelve shoes in the kitchen (i.e. six pairs) and Elizabeth notes with disdain and superiority how untidy her kitchen is. Mrs Rigley goes to the pub to fetch her husband, while Elizabeth waits in Mrs Rigley's house in case the children wake up. It is interesting to note that Mrs Rigley is prepared to go inside the pub to fetch her husband – an action Elizabeth sees as beneath her. As soon as Elizabeth leaves with Mr Rigley, his wife rushes next door to spread the gossip about Walter Bates being missing.

Mr Rigley

A fellow miner, Mr Rigley kindly checks the local pubs in an effort to find Walter and discovers that Walter has had an accident – news he passes on to Walter's mother.

Elizabeth's Father

Elizabeth's father is a bearded, cheerful railway engine driver who brings Elizabeth news that he is to re-marry because "It's no sort of life for a man of my years, to sit at my own hearth like a stranger. And if I'm going to marry again it may as well be soon as late – what does it matter to anybody?" He is obviously widowed and slightly concerned that he is marrying too quickly after his first wife's death. Elizabeth does not really reassure him about this, and, although she brings him a cup of tea and a hunk of bread and butter, her attitude to him is quite cold. He apologizes for not coming to see her the previous Sunday, but Elizabeth's reply – "I didn't expect you" – makes him wince. It is Elizabeth's father who first gossips about Walter and tells Elizabeth that Walter had been heard boasting that he would be indulging in a drinking spree that night. Elizabeth's father condemns his actions clearly and sarcastically: "… it's a nice thing when a man can do nothing with his money but make a beast of himself."

Language and Imagery

The dialect and phonetic spelling that Lawrence allows some of the characters to use adds a realistic flavour to the story. It also reveals character because Elizabeth Bates speaks throughout the story in Standard English, showing her social superiority to the community of which she is a part and her aspiration for a better life. Lawrence's use of local dialect and accent does not simply add realism – it increases our sense of Elizabeth's isolation within the mining community.

Lawrence's own writing is precise and he makes frequent use of simile and metaphor. His opening description of the mining community (which is examined in more detail below under Setting) shows the coal mine and its environment having a negative effect on nature and on the humans who have the misfortune to live and work there. Apart from the pollution coming from the coal mine, the human beings in the landscape are threatened too: the raspberry canes from which John emerges are 'like whips'. It is almost as if the humans in the story are about to disappear: the miners walk home 'like shadows' and later in the story Elizabeth puts a dustpan outside and returns to the house 'like a shadow'.

The animal and natural imagery that Lawrence uses suggests very broadly that the characters are part are part of a larger and very unpredictable cycle of life and death. John is compared to a frog when he crawls out from beneath the sofa' Elizabeth predicts that when his mates carry Walter home drunk he will be 'like a log'. Walter, according to one of the miners who carries the stretcher with Walter's corpse on it, says he was caught like a mouse in a mouse trap – a simile that might apply to all the families and miners forced to live in the pit village. Walter's mother's tears are like 'drops from wet leaves' – Lawrence suggests she is weeping so copiously because she thinks it is expected of her. The unborn child is 'like ice' in Elizabeth as the truth of Walter's death hits her and the financial difficulties she will face become apparent. At critical points in the story – firstly out of anger at Walter and then out of dread and fear – Elizabeth's heart seizes up and fills with tension. Finally in the last sentence of the story, life and death are personified as Elizabeth's two masters.

At the same time, perhaps because he is writing about a milieu he knows so well, Lawrence writes a convincingly realistic story about working class life from the efforts to keep the fire going, the simple, filling meal, the rats in the yard and the single candle which illuminates the laying out of Walter's corpse at the end of the story.

Lawrence's use of dialogue is also very succinct: he manages to convey a lot of information through small breaks of dialogue: the miners who bring the corpse are sympathetic but fairly taciturn because there is nothing they can say which might console Elizabeth. The longest speeches are by Elizabeth when she is complaining to the children about Walter's behaviour, and Walter's mother when she is remembering what Walter was like as a child.

Finally Lawrence's description of Elizabeth's highly complex feelings are dealt with superbly by Lawrence's analytical prose. He leads us as readers to Elizabeth's epiphany and her realization that she was partly responsible for never accepting or truly knowing the man that Walter was. This realization comes to Elizabeth slowly and incrementally, and Lawrence's prose guides the reader adeptly through her tumultuous feelings and thoughts.

Prolepsis and Foreshadowing

Lawrence uses both prolepsis and foreshadowing in the story and, while the techniques are similar, they are not the same at all. Foreshadowing is a moment in the story when a character says or thinks something that will come true later in the story or which hints at something which will come true. For example, at the end of the first chapter Lawrence writes of Elizabeth, "Meantime her anger was tinged with fear" – anger that Walter is drinking in the pub tempered by fear that he has had an accident in the mine.

On the other hand, prolepsis is a form of irony – proleptic irony. This works in the following way: something happens or something is said which turns out to be ironic in the light of later events. On several occasions Elizabeth talks about how his mates will have to carry him home from the pub dead drunk and she states that he can sleep on the floor where they drop him: these are examples of prolepsis because they are ironically wrong as we read the rest of the story, because, although Walter is carried home and left on the parlour floor, he is dead, suffocated in the mine. The following quotation from Elizabeth is a perfect example of prolepsis:

Twenty minutes to six! ….eh, he'll not come now till they bring him. There he'll stick! But he needn't come rolling in here in his pit-dirt, for I won't wash him. He can lie on the floor.

And a little later, "They'll bring him when he does come – like a log". The irony lies in the partial truth of Elizabeth's words – they do carry him into the parlour and, in fact, she does end up washing him because he is dead. It is irony because she is wrong and proleptic irony because we only recognize it in hindsight as we look back over the story or read it for a second time.

Setting

The setting of 'Odour of Chrysanthemums' is bleak and bare. In his opening paragraph Lawrence shows the clash between the mechanized world of the mine and the natural world. The railway engine startles a colt and forces a young woman to get out of its way and shelter next to a hedge. The pit-bank is described as having 'flames like red sores licking its ashy sides' making it sound like a wounded beast. The fields are 'dreary and forsaken'. The oak is 'withered', the cabbages are 'ragged', the chrysanthemums are 'dishevelled' and even Elizabeth's son is lost in the darkness. The miners trooping homewards are 'shadows'. Nature seems to be hostile to humanity: the Bates's cottage is - 'A large bony vine clutched at the house, as if to claw down the tiled roof.' The Bates's house is small with a kitchen where they eat, live and play, and a front room or parlour which is used for special occasions – such as the laying out of a dead body. Presumably there are two bedrooms upstairs. The yard is infested with rats. The Bates are poor which makes Walter's wasting money on beer even more foolhardy. Most of the story takes place in darkness because it is late afternoon and twilight when the story begins and ten o' clock at night when the men bring Walter's body to the house. The darkness also reflects the tragic outcome of the story and the hard lives that the characters face in the pit village.

Themes

Poverty

The Bates are a poor family: working class workers were paid very badly during this era and trade unionism was in its relative infancy, so the workers found it hard to negotiate for better pay: however, Lawrence has no interest in this side of his story. The poverty of the family is clear and must add to the strains in the marriage when Walter wastes so much money in the pub. Signs of poverty are John's clothes: some of Walter's old clothes cut down to fit his five-year-old frame. The children's evening meal consists of large pieces of toasted bread – cheap but filling, followed by batter pudding – another cheap but filling dish. The cottage they live in is small and has no electricity – light comes from candles, the fire and oil lamps – one of which Elizabeth lights in the course of the meal. In the garden there are signs that they grow their own vegetables to save money – the cabbages and the raspberry canes – and they keep chickens in a fowl house – for eggs and meat.

Conflict and Divisions

Throughout the story Lawrence presents aspects of life or areas of life which are in conflict with each other, and these dichotomies centre around his thematic concerns.

One conflict is between man and his environment which we have touched on in writing about setting. The bleak environment of the pit village is presented as hostile to man and to nature, and also disrupts the human relationship with nature. The miners trooping homeward are mere 'shadows' and their lives are blighted by the coal mine; Walter's death in the mine could be seen as symbolic of the way the mine dominates and pollutes the landscape. Working in the coal mine is dangerous, dirty and physically-exhausting work with the constant threat of injury or death. Nature too is ruined by the demands of industrialized society as Lawrence's opening description shows so vividly.

Lawrence presents an element of social class conflict too in Elizabeth's sense of her own superiority to her neighbours. Ironically the neighbours Elizabeth looks down on are warm, friendly people who gladly give up their time to help Elizabeth in her search for Walter. But we might note that Mrs Rigley speak to Elizabeth 'in a tone tinged with respect'. Elizabeth is still working class, but she seems aspirational and resents living where she does – 'this dirty hole' – and we can see that she is trying to bring up John and Annie with a sense of decorum and good behaviour.

The conflict between men and women is epitomized in the Bates's marriage, and it was a conflict that Lawrence often returned to in his novels and other stories. For most of the story we are encouraged, by

Lawrence's narrative point of view, to see Walter as the problem – wasting his wages in prolonged drinking sessions and neglecting his wife and children as he does so. Indeed, Elizabeth could be said to be suffocating in her marriage to Walter, although Lawrence never uses any imagery to suggest that. However, the end of the story leads to Elizabeth's insight that she is as much to blame for any failings in their marriage as Walter was. They have produced three children but – despite the physical intimacy that involved – they were strangers to each other:

There had been nothing between them, and yet they had come together, exchanging their nakedness repeatedly. Each time he had taken her, they had been two isolated beings, far apart as now.... And her soul died in her for fear: she knew she had never seen him, he had never seen her, they had met in the dark and fought in the dark, not knowing whom they met nor whom they fought.

Elizabeth's epiphany allows her to see that she was partly to blame for the failings in her marriage: 'She had denied him what he was – she saw it now. She had refused him as herself – she saw it now.' Most of Lawrence's novels deal with relationships between men and women, and one phrase from the last quotation above stands out – 'in the dark' – Lawrence could justifiably be said to be in favour of greater openness and light in dealing with sexual and emotional matters between men and women. This understanding leads to empathy on Elizabeth's part, but also an awareness that they are now separated for ever by death. And so the story ends with a major division – that between the living and the dead.

Most of the story takes place in the dark, but Lawrence uses light as a contrast throughout the story. The light in the kitchen comes from the fire until Elizabeth lights the central oil lamp. The family eat their meal with their faces in darkness – John 'was almost lost in darkness' and his face is 'a dusty mark on the shadow'. By contrast, the Prince of Wales pub looks 'warm and bright'. John often complains about the room being too dark, and we learn he is like his father in this respect, while Annie is transfixed by the brightness and colour of the fire itself. However, fire carries a potential danger – while Mrs Rigley goes to get her husband from the pub she asks Elizabeth to wait for her to ensure that 'th' childer doesn't come downstairs and set theirselves afire.' In a story that revolves around a death, Lawrence uses light and dark to foreshadow in a very general way Walter's passage to the ultimate darkness – death.

The contrast between the living and the dead is also central to the story. In practical terms – a widow with three children to bring up – Walter's death is a disaster for the family. In addition, Elizabeth is astonished at the transformation that death brings: as they attempt to clothe Walter's corpse at the end of the story

He was so heavy and inert. A terrible dread ripped her all the while: that he could be so heavy and utterly inert, unresponsive, apart. The horror of the distance between them was almost too much for her – it was so infinite a gap she must look across.

However, in terms of what Elizabeth learns about her marriage (albeit in retrospect) and what the readers perceive about the awful finality of death, the whole story could be said to be building up to the final sentence:

She knew she submitted to life, which was her immediate master. But from death, her ultimate master, she winced with fear and shame.

To submit to something means to surrender and Elizabeth is caught as effectively as Walter is in the mining accident – 'like a mouse-trap' – because she has two, soon to be three, children to bring up, but her submission to life means that she is willing to face up to her responsibilities.

The Motif of Chrysanthemums

Apart from being in the title, chrysanthemums recur throughout the short story. Chrysanthemums come in thousands of varieties and are valued for the variety of their petal structure and the bright, vivid nature of their blooms, particularly as they bloom in late summer and the autumn. Their scent is more variable and some chrysanthemums have a musty, pungent, almost acrid smell. In most European countries chrysanthemums are associated with funerals and, therefore, death.

John scatters chrysanthemum petals across the path at the start of the story and is reprimanded by his mother because it looks nasty; Elizabeth places a sprig of chrysanthemums in her apron band which Elizabeth enthuses over – although she is told she is being 'silly' by her mother and Elizabeth bursts out bitterly when Annie says they smell beautiful:

"'No," she said, "not to me. It was chrysanthemums when I married him, and chrysanthemums when you were born, and the first time they ever brought him home drunk, he'd got brown chrysanthemums in his button-hole."'

Later in the story when the men carry Walter's body into the parlour one of the men knocks over a vase of chrysanthemums on the table breaking the vase – it is almost a symbolic gesture summing up the tragedy of Walter's death, the Bates's unhappy marriage and the difficult and poverty-stricken life that Elizabeth can look forward to as a widow with three children under ten.

The Ending

There is no doubt that faced with Walter's naked body and engaged in the act of washing it, Elizabeth comes to realize how little she knew her husband, how little they knew each other and that if their marriage was a failure it was the fault of both of them. She is also overawed by the enormity and finality of death, knowing that she must live on in order to look after the children. Some readers have suggested that the final scene in the parlour resembles the paintings in the pietà tradition: paintings depicting Jesus being washed by his mother and Mary Magdelene after his death on the cross (like the one alongside). We are not sure Lawrence intended this, and it certainly does not transform Walter into a Christ-like figure, but it does make clear his role as innocent victim – a victim (like the landscape) of industrialization and mechanization.

Printed in Great Britain
by Amazon

64533214R00031